SCENE BY SCENE
COMPARATIVE WORKBOOK HL17

The Spinning Heart

by Donal Ryan

Theme/Issue - Relationships

Literary Genre

General Vision and Viewpoint

Scene by Scene
11 Millfield, Enniskerry
Wicklow, Ireland.
www.scenebysceneguides.com

info@scenebysceneguides.com

The Spinning Heart Comparative Workbook HL17 by Amy Farrell. —1st ed.
ISBN 978-1-910949-46-7

The Spinning Heart Comparative Study Workbook

This workbook is designed to help Leaving Certificate English students become familiar with the Comparative Study modes and to understand how each mode may be applied to *The Spinning Heart*.

The Comparative Study Modes at Higher Level for 2017 are:

Theme/Issue

The theme covered in this workbook is Relationships. This theme can be applied to any relationship in a text and covers love, marriage, friendship and family bonds.

Consider the complexities of relationships and the impact they have on characters' lives.

Literary Genre

This mode refers to the way the story is told.

Consider aspects of narration such as the manner and style of narration, characterisation, setting, tension, literary techniques, etc.

The General Vision and Viewpoint

This mode refers to the author's outlook or view of life and how this viewpoint is represented in the text.

Consider whether the text is bright or dark, optimistic or pessimistic, uplifting or bleak, etc.

How Does it Work?

This workbook has three parts, one each for Theme/Issue (our chosen theme for study is Relationships), Literary Genre and General Vision and Viewpoint. Each part has three sections: Know the Text, Know the Mode and Compare the Texts.

Know The Text

These questions are on *The Spinning Heart* text and refer specifically to this novel. Through answering these questions you will get to know the text well, while also getting a feel for the Comparative Study mode the questions relate to.

Know the Mode

These questions use 'mode' specific terms and phrases and are intended to help prepare you for tackling exam questions. They focus on the mode itself, rather than the text you have studied. You apply your knowledge of the text to the mode in question.

Compare the Texts

These questions ask you to compare your texts under specific aspects of each mode. It is important that you get used to the idea of comparing sand contrasting your chosen texts, as this is what the Comparative Study is all about. It is good practice to think about your texts in terms of their similarities and differences within each mode.

This approach is designed to prevent 'drift' between modes and focuses on analysis and personal response, rather than summary.

Theme/Issue - Know the Text

1	What are your first impressions of Bobby's relationship with his father, Frank?

2	What was it like for Bobby growing up?

3 What sort of father is Frank?
Why does he treat his son this way?

4 How do you respond to reading about the way Bobby was treated by his father?

5 How does Bobby **feel** about his father?

6 How well do Bobby and Frank **communicate**, interact and understand one another?

7 What **problems** or weaknesses can you identify in their relationship?

8 Can you identify any **strengths** or positives in their relationship?

9 In what ways did Frank hurt his son and damage their relationship?
How has Bobby been affected by this?

10 When you first learned of Frank's death, did you think Bobby had murdered him? Explain.

11   Why doesn't Bobby protest his innocence?

12   What did you learn about Bobby and Frank's relationship from reading Frank's chapter?

13 Does Bobby's relationship with his father shock or surprise you in any way?

14 What insights do you get from reading about Bobby and Frank's relationship?

15 What view of Frank do the local people have? Does he have good relationships with the people of the community?

16 What view of Bobby do the local people have? Does he have good relationships with the people of the community?

17 Does Bobby have a good relationship with his wife, Triona?

18 How well do Bobby and Triona **communicate**, interact and understand one another?

19 What **strengths** do you see in Bobby and Triona's marriage?

20 What **weaknesses** or problems do you see in Bobby and Triona's marriage?

21 What threatens to damage Bobby and Triona's relationship?

22 Is this a positive or negative relationship?

23 As the story ends, do you feel you know everything about Bobby and Triona's marriage?

24 Does their marriage bring Bobby and Triona happiness?

Theme/Issue - Know the Mode

25 Are relationships in this text generally **positive** (warm, supportive, nurturing, genuine) or **negative** (cold, cruel, destructive, false)?

26 What makes relationships in this text complicated and **difficult**?

27 What would **improve** relationships in this text?

28 How do relationships **change** during the story?

How do relationships **change** during the story?

29 What did **you learn** about relationships from reading this novel?

30

Are relationships **portrayed realistically** in this text? Make use of examples to support the points you make.

31

Are relationships in this story **interesting** and **involving**?

32

Did anything about the theme of relationships in this text **shock, upset** or **unsettle** you?

33 What is the **most signficant relationship** in this text?
What makes it so significant and important?

34 Do relationships in this story bring characters **happiness** or **sorrow**?

35 Choose **key moments** from this story that highlight relationships in the text.

Theme/Issue - Compare the Texts

36 Were relationships in *The Spinning Heart* more positive and supportive than the relationships in your other texts? Give specific examples.

37 Rank the relationships you have studied in your various texts from most positive to most negative. Add a note to explain your choices.

38 Were relationships in *The Spinning Heart* the most engaging and interesting that you have studied? Explain your choice.

39 Rank the relationships you have studied in your various texts from most interesting to least interesting. Add a note to explain your choices.

40 Did you **learn most** about the theme of relationships from this text or another text on your comparative course?

41 What **similarities** do you notice in the theme of relationships in this text and your other comparative texts?

42 What **differences** do you notice in the theme of relationships in this text and your other comparative texts?

Literary Genre - Know the Text

43 How is this story told? (Consider the novel format).

44 Why is the story told in this way?
What is the effect of this?

45 Do you like the **changing narrators** for each chapter? Explain your view.

46 Comment on the **language** the speakers use.

47 How does the **rural Irish setting** add to the story?

48 Which accounts did you find particularly moving or **emotional**?

49 Which accounts did you find humorous or **entertaining**?

50 Which speakers would you like to have heard more from? What interested you in their stories?

51 Bobby Mahon is the opening speaker.
How does the author **develop** this character?

52 Is the death of Frank Mahon an **unexpected twist**? How did you react to this development?

53   What other developments made this an **exciting** story?

54   Did you think Bobby had killed his father when you first learned of Frank's death?
What led you to believe this?

55 Why does Donal Ryan make use of conflicting accounts and **rumours** as he tells the story?

56 Apart from the plot, what other aspects of the novel made you want to read on?

57 Is this a novel about family, relationships, our private selves, or something else?

58 Were any voices absent from the story? Were there characters whose stories remained untold?

59 In a review of this novel, *The Guardian* said, "the testimony of his (Ryan's) characters rings rich and true." Do you agree with this assessment?

Literary Genre - Know the Mode

60

Did **you** enjoy the **storyline** of the text?
Was it exciting/compelling/tense/emotional?
Why/why not?

61

Is there just one **plot** or many plots?
What connections can you make between the storylines?

62 What three things interested **you** most in the story?

63 Are **characters** vivid, realistic and well-developed?

64 Do **you** empathise or **identify** with any character(s)?
Did you become involved in this story or care about the characters? Use examples.

65 Who was your **favourite character**?
What aspects of this character did you enjoy?

66 Consider Bobby Mahon as the novel's **hero**. What made Bobby a **memorable** or **interesting** character?

67 Who was your **least favourite character**? What aspects of this character did you dislike? What made them a memorable or interesting character?

68 Is the story humorous or tragic, romantic or realistic? Explain using examples.

69 To what **genre** does it belong?
What aspects of this genre did **you** enjoy?
Is it Romance, Thriller, Horror, Action/Adventure, Historical, Fantasy, Science-fiction, Satire, etc.?

70 How does the author create **suspense**, **high emotion** and **excitement** in the text? What **techniques** does he use to good advantage?

71 Consider the author's use of **tension** and **resolution** in the novel. What are the major **tensions/problems/conflicts** in the text? Are they **resolved** or not?

72 Did the author make use of any striking patterns of **imagery** or **symbols** to add to the story?

73 How does the author make use of the **unexpected** in this text? What did this add to the story? (Think about key moments here.)

74   What is the **climax** (high point) of the story?

75   What did **you** think of this moment?
How did it make **you feel**?

76   Comment on the **language** of the novel.
How does dialect add to the story? What does the
honesty of each account bring to the story?

77   Comment on the **pacing** of the novel.
How does this add to the story?

78 Comment on the **setting** of the novel.
Consider time, place, and specific locations, as well as the backdrop of rural Ireland. How does setting add to your understanding of the characters and their story?

79

Was anything about this novel moving or emotional?

Think of moments in the novel that you responded to. What made them moving? How did this add to the story?

80 On a scale of one to ten, how much did you enjoy the **ending**? What was satisfying/unsatisfying about it? Was anything left unanswered?

81 The experiences of seeing a play, reading a novel and viewing a film are very different.
What aspects of the **novel form** worked well in this story, in your opinion?

82 What did **you** like about **the way** the story was told?
*Mention aspects of storytelling and literary techniques that **you** found enjoyable. Refer to key moments.*

83 Identify **key moments** in the novel that illustrate Literary Genre (the way the story is told). Clearly **define literary techniques/aspects of narrative** in your analysis.

Literary Genre - Compare the Texts

84 Did **you** like the way this story was told more than your other comparative texts?
State what you enjoyed most about each.

85

Is *The Spinning Heart* more **exciting** than your other texts?
Consider tension, pacing, suspense, conflict and the unexpected.

86 Are **characters** more engaging in this novel than in your other texts?
Refer to each of your texts in your answer.

87 Is the **setting** more effective in telling this story than in your other texts?
Refer to each of your texts in your answer.

88 Is this story more **unpredictable** than your other texts?
Refer to each of your texts in your answer.

89 Did this novel have greater **emotional power** than your other texts?
Was emotional power created in a more interesting way here or in a different text?

90 What **similarities** do you notice in the Literary Genre of this novel and your other comparative texts?
Mention specific aspects of narrative.

91 What **differences** do you notice in the Literary Genre of this novel and your other comparative texts?
Mention specific aspects of narrative.

General Vision and Viewpoint - Know the Text

92 What **problems** does Donal Ryan focus on in this novel?

93 A number of accounts recount the **destructive side of alcohol** in Ireland.
How does this contribute to Ryan's General Vision and Viewpoint?

94 How does the **recession**, **unemployment** and **financial strain** affect the mood of the novel?

95 There are a number of **dark characters** in this novel. Who are they and how do they add to the mood of the story?

96 Some characters remain **hopeful** and optimistic in the face of their troubles. Who are these **positive characters**? How does their take on life influence the General Vision and Viewpoint of the story?

97 Triona believes completely in her husband's goodness and never doubts him. What does this belief in Bobby add to the outlook of the story?

98 Characters in this novel struggle to tell each other how they really feel. How does this affect the General Vision and Viewpoint of the text?

99 Some characters appear hurt or in pain. Who are these characters? How does their **suffering** contribute to the General Vision and Viewpoint?

100 How do references to **violence** and **death** contribute to the novel's outlook?

101 Do you want Bobby to clear his name and live happily ever after? Do you think this is likely? Explain your view.

102 Dylan is rescued from his kidnappers unharmed. How does this development contribute to the General Vision and Viewpoint of the text?

103 Overall, what is the **mood** of this novel? Use examples to illustrate your ideas.

104 What aspects of this story did you find **saddening**?

105 What aspects of this story did you find **uplifting**?

106 Does this novel have a **happy ending**?
How does this impact on the General Vision and Viewpoint?

107 What is Donal Ryan telling us about life in this story?
What is Donal Ryan's message?
Is his outlook positive or negative, in your view?

General Vision and Viewpoint - Know the Mode

108 Identify bright/hopeful/optimistic aspects of the novel.

109 Identify dark/hopeless/pessimistic aspects of the novel.

110 Is this text **optimistic** or **pessimistic**? Explain. *Consider characters' happiness, imagery, atmosphere, future prospects, etc.*

111 On a scale of one to ten, how optimistic is this text?

112

Identify the **aspects of life** that the author concentrates on.
Are they positive or negative?
Consider unhappiness, isolation, violence, love, etc.

113 What **comments** do characters make on their **society** and the problems they're facing?

114 Are characters happy or unhappy?

115 What makes characters in this story happy and fulfilled?

116 What makes characters in this story unhappy and unfulfilled?

117 Are **relationships** destructive or nurturing? What do they reveal about life, as we see characters supported/thwarted in their efforts to grow/mature?

118

Are **imagery** and **language** bright or dark in the text? (Tone of the text)

119 What is the **mood** of this text?

120 What does this story **teach us about life**?

What do we learn about life's hardships? Are struggles overcome? Is determination rewarded? Is life difficult or joyful?

121 How do you **feel** as you read this novel?
Refer to key moments to anchor your answer.

122   How do you **feel** at the **end**?

123 Are **questions** raised by the text **resolved** by the end?
Are they resolved **happily** or **unhappily**?

124 Are **you hopeful** or **despairing** regarding the prospects for human **happiness** in this story? *Are characters likely to be happy?*

125 Identify the **key moments** in the novel that illustrate the General Vision and Viewpoint of the text.

95

General Vision and Viewpoint - Compare the Texts

126 Is life happier for characters in this story than in your other comparative texts? Explain.

127 Do characters in this text face more obstacles and difficulties than in your other texts?
Who struggles most?

128 Are characters in this text **rewarded more** for their struggles than in your other texts?
By overcoming adversity, do they achieve true happiness and contentment in a way that is not realised in your other texts?

129 Is this the brightest, most hopeful and triumphant text you have studied? Explain why its message is more or less positive than your other texts.

130 Which of your chosen texts was the bleakest and most upsetting or depressing?
Explain why it was more negative than your other texts.
What made them more positive?

131 Plot your three texts on a scale of one to ten, from darkest (most pessimistic) to brightest (most optimistic). Add points to explain their position.

132 What **similarities** do you notice in the General Vision and Viewpoint of this text and your other comparative texts?

133 What **differences** do you notice in the General Vision and Viewpoint of this text and your other comparative texts?